D0280263

level **2**

# What Animals Eat

WITHDRAWN

Brenda Stones

**KINGFISHER**

**KINGFISHER**

First published 2012 by Kingfisher
an imprint of Macmillan Children's Books
a division of Macmillan Publishers Limited
20 New Wharf Road, London N1 9RR
Basingstoke and Oxford
Associated companies throughout the world
www.panmacmillan.com

Series editor: Heather Morris
Literacy consultant: Hilary Horton

ISBN: 978-0-7534-3054-5
Copyright © Macmillan Publishers Ltd 2012

All rights reserved. No part of this publication may be
reproduced, stored in or introduced into a retrieval system,
or transmitted, in any form or by any means (electronic,
mechanical, photocopying, recording or otherwise),
without the prior written permission of the publisher.
Any person who does any unauthorized act in relation
to this publication may be liable to criminal
prosecution and civil claims for damages.

9 8 7 6 5 4 3 2 1

1TR/1011/WKT/UNTD/105MA

A CIP catalogue record for this book is available
from the British Library.

Printed in China

This book is sold subject to the condition that it shall not, by way
of trade or otherwise, be lent, resold, hired out, or otherwise
circulated without the publisher's prior consent in any form of
binding or cover other than that in which it is published and without
a similar condition including this condition being imposed on the
subsequent purchaser.

**TOWER HAMLETS**
**LIBRARIES**

| 91000001091461 | |
| --- | --- |
| Bertrams | 12/01/2012 |
| J591 | £3.99 |
| THCUB | TH11001852 |

Picture credits
The Publisher would like to thank the following for permission to reproduce
their material. Every care has been taken to trace copyright holders.
Top = t; Bottom = b; Centre = c; Left = l; Right = r
Cover Shutterstock(SS); Pages 4 SS/Christina Richards; 5t SS/neelsky; 5b SS/Kemeo; 6 SS/Johan Swanepoel;
7t SS/Michael Zysman; 7b SS/Gerrit de Vries; 8 SS/David Maska; 9t SS/Ivica Jandrijevic; 9b SS/Mark Schwettmann;
10t Alamy/Donald Mammoser; 10b SS/2009fotofriends; 11 SS/Redwood; 12 SS/Gerrit de Vries; 13 SS/Eric Gevaert;
14 Photolibrary/Gerard Soury; 15 SS/Crumpler; 16t Photolibrary/Buddy Mays; 16b SS/Wolfgang Staib; 17 SS/Dr Morely
Read; 18 SS/Monkey Business Images; 19 SS/Gusev Mikhail Evgenivitch; 20–21 Photoshot/John Shaw/NHPA;
21 Photoshot/T Kitchin & V Hurst/NHPA; 22 SS/Edwin Verin; 23 SS/Floridastock; 24 SS/NatUlrich;
27 Photolibrary/Daniel J. Cox; 29 Photolibrary/Paul Goldstein; 31 FLPA/Reinhard Dirschel.

# Contents

# Animal diets

Did you know that different animals eat different foods? There are three kinds of **diet** for animals.

Animals that eat plants are called **herbivores**. Deer are big herbivores. Rabbits are small herbivores.

Animals that eat meat are called **carnivores**. Cats, tigers and lions are all carnivores.

Animals that eat both plants and meat are called **omnivores**. Chickens and apes are omnivores.

# Elephants

The elephant is the largest animal on land. It has to eat for 18 hours a day to get all the food it needs.

Elephants eat grass, twigs, fruits and tree bark.

# Giraffes

The giraffe is the tallest animal in the world. It eats leaves from the tops of trees.

The giraffe's long neck can reach up high. But it's a long way down to drink!

# Cows

Cows eat grass and weeds, like this dandelion.

When it is cold, the farmer brings the cows into the barn to eat grain and hay.

# Sheep and goats

Sheep and goats eat grass too. They eat early in the morning and late in the afternoon.

Cows, sheep and goats chew their food many times to get all the goodness out of it.

# Rabbits

In the wild, rabbits eat grass. They also eat carrots and other hard vegetables, which are good for their teeth.

This pet rabbit is eating a mix of food.

# Squirrels

Squirrels eat nuts and acorns.
They also eat tree bark, which
they pull off with their sharp claws.

Squirrels store nuts underground.
They eat them in the winter,
when food is hard
to find.

# Lions

Lions live in Africa. They hunt and eat other large animals.

Animals who hunt are called **predators**. The food they kill is their **prey**.

# Sharks

Sharks eat every kind of meat they can find in the sea. They hunt fish, crabs and sea birds.

Sharks have many rows of very sharp teeth to catch their prey.

# Eagles

Eagles are **birds of prey**. They eat rabbits, snakes and smaller birds.

Eagles fly high in the sky looking for their prey. When they see a small animal, they dive down and catch it with their claws.

# Frogs

Frogs eat snails, worms and flies. They catch them with their sticky tongues. Frogs eat on land.

Baby frogs are called tadpoles. They live in water and only eat plants.

# Spiders

Spiders eat flies, wasps, moths and other insects. They spin a web to trap their prey. Then they kill it with poison and eat it.

# People

People can eat almost anything!
We can eat meat, fish, vegetables,
grains and fats.

People who do not eat meat are
called **vegetarians**.

# Monkeys

Monkeys and apes belong to the same family as humans. They eat fruits, berries, leaves and insects.

# Bears

Bears sleep in the winter. When they wake up in the spring they are very hungry! This grizzly bear is catching a fish.

In the spring, bears eat sheep, deer and fish. In the summer they eat nuts, grass and berries, like this black bear.

# Seagulls

At sea, seagulls eat fish, **shellfish** and small sea plants.

On land, they pick up whatever they can find, even fish and chips or ice-cream!

# Woodpeckers

The woodpecker taps
a hole in the bark
with its strong **beak**.
Then it picks out
ants and beetles
with its long,
sticky tongue.

The woodpecker
also eats fruits,
seeds and nuts.

# Food chains

Food chains show how animals get their **energy**. The energy starts with the sun.

Sunlight makes
plants grow.

Animals eat
the plants.

Big animals eat
the little animals.

Animals eat plants or other animals
for energy to live and grow.

# In the forest

Here is a food chain in the forest.

The sun makes the leaf grow.

The beetle eats the leaf.

The mouse eats the beetle.

The owl eats the mouse.

# In the grasslands

Here is a food chain in the grasslands.

The sun makes the grass grow.

The zebra eats the grass.

The lion eats the zebra.

# In the sea

Here is a food chain in the sea.

Sunlight makes
seaweed grow.

The fish eats
the seaweed.

The octopus
eats the fish.

The shark eats the octopus.

# Glossary

**beak** a bird's sharp mouth

**birds of prey** birds that kill other animals to eat

**carnivores** animals that eat other animals

**diet** the kind of food animals eat

**energy** power to move or grow

**herbivores** animals that eat plants

**omnivores** animals that eat meat and plants

**predators** animals that hunt and kill other animals for food

**prey** animals that are hunted by predators

**shellfish** small sea animals with a hard shell

**vegetarians** people who don't eat meat

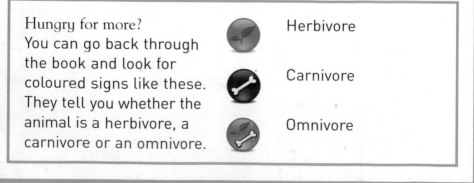

Hungry for more?
You can go back through the book and look for coloured signs like these. They tell you whether the animal is a herbivore, a carnivore or an omnivore.

Herbivore

Carnivore

Omnivore